DON'T SKIP THE PROCESS

MAKING LIFE'S CHALLENGES

WORK FOR YOU

HERBERT C. BROWN

DON'T SKIP THE PROCESS

DON'T SKIP THE PROCESS

The opinions expressed in the manuscript are solely the opinions of the author and do not represent the opinions or thoughts of the publisher. The author has represented and warranted full ownership and/or legal right to publish all the material in this book.

All scriptures quotations, unless otherwise indicated, were taken from The King James or NIV versions of the Holy Bible via www.biblegateway.com

Author: Herbert C. Brown

Cover Design: Danetta Barney

Editor: Jeanette Jones

Don't Skip the Process, Making Life's Challenges work for You

ISBN-13: 978-1508866398

Inspirational and Motivational

Printed in the United States of America

DEDICATION

My Lord and Savior Jesus Christ, my wife
Tracey of 30 years of marriage, not only my wife
but best friend and my two daughters Kayla and
Eboni who also support my goals and
encourage me.

To my late Mother Patricia Ann King Brown who
taught me the true meaning of character and
integrity and to my late sister Barbara Curtis
(gone too soon) and to my brothers and sisters
for always being close even when far apart
(living wise).

To my brother-in-law's, sister-in-law, nieces,
nephews and all family, my mother-in-law
Loretta and father-in-law John who have always
been there for us.

ACKNOWLEGEMENTS

I would like to thank everyone who encouraged me and supported me in my efforts to finish this book. Thank you to my sisters Jeanette Jones (author of God's Adjust'n My Wings) and Danetta Barney (author of Sticks & Stones & Butterflies). I truly appreciate your guidance and help through this process.

A special thank you goes to you, the readers. May this book richly bless your lives and place you in a better position to finish whatever you have started or plan to start.

INTRODUCTION

This book is inspired by personal events and from my professional experience in law enforcement. As you read this book, I think you will find a message that speaks to you and can help improve whatever situation you may be going through.

Writing this book has been a labor of love for me because I like to help people. It is my hope that you will find a message that speaks to you and motivates you to move in a positive direction despite whatever challenges you face. Success doesn't happen without some failures along the way. This means you have to prepare yourself to continue fighting for what's important and not give up because of disappointments.

DON'T SKIP THE PROCESS

Look at it this way, no scientist, inventor or athlete ever achieves their objective by quitting and going home. Success comes from hard work, endurance, and determination. If you believe it you can achieve it.

The dictionary defines "process" as a series of actions or steps taken in order to achieve a particular end. I believe "process" also describes the various stages of life we must all go through as we develop from childhood to adulthood. It is tempting to try and skip the unpleasant parts of life and fast forward to the next phase. That's simply human nature. Haven't you heard young children say, "I wish I was a grown-up," especially when things didn't go their way? In their young minds grown-ups have it made; they appear to have ultimate control of whatever decisions they make.

DON'T SKIP THE PROCESS

Children think grown-ups can eat as much candy or ice cream as they want, when they want, and without asking permission. They don't understand that this type of freedom also comes with responsibility and failing to use it wisely can result in negative consequences. As adults we know how important self-discipline is in making decisions. Eating or drinking too much sugar can lead to a mouth full of cavities and even diabetes. So children need guidance and balance in their lives until they mature physically and mentally. On the opposite end, there are adults who remain fixated on the past and waste time wishing they could re-live their youth. There is a time and a season for everything. Instead of living our lives and wishing for something that cannot be regained, we should focus on what's in front of us. If you enjoy the moment as it happens I the present you won't have regrets for letting that time slip away.

DON'T SKIP THE PROCESS

Everyone has the potential to live their life to the "fullest," and reach their aspirations. It begins with having dreams and goals you would like to fulfil. Next, you have to develop a game plan or a strategy for accomplishing your goals. Those who fail to plan; plan to fail. That's because it takes actual work and perseverance to "turn" dreams into reality. It is also extremely important that you develop a relationship with Jesus Christ and read and study the Bible. Life is challenging. Sometimes even the best of plans don't work out, but you shouldn't let that discourage you or stop you from achieving your dreams. When you accept Jesus Christ as your Lord and Savior you know that one of the most powerful weapons you have is "prayer." When you keep an open line of communication with Jesus, through prayer and meditation it strengthens you spiritually and physically. Believers know that though the power of prayer and faith they can withstand life's challenges and overcome them. It is impossible to please God without faith. (Hebrews 11:6 KJV). When you have faith in God, nothing is impossible to achieve. (Matthew 19:26 KJV). NOW faith is the substance of things hoped for, the evidence of things not seen. (Hebrews 11:1 KJV).

Throughout this book you will find various Bible verses and scripture passages. They are intended to share Biblical principles and promises that will provide guidance and support. Reading and meditating on these scriptures will help you to navigate through life in good times and in bad times. You will also find a section to take notes or write down your thoughts at the end of each chapter.

TABLE OF CONTENTS

FINDING PURPOSE IN THE PROCESS

1

Everything seems to be rush, rush, move, move in today's society. Everyone appears hard-wired to move at a fast pace, regardless of the work to be completed. No one has time anymore to follow through with completing each step in a particular process (or so we tell ourselves). There is no doubt that time is precious, but it's also important to get things done right. Sometimes moving too quickly and avoiding steps actually costs us more time in the long run.

DON'T SKIP THE PROCESS

Life, itself is a process. You have different stages beginning with conception where the egg is awaiting the process necessary to develop into a baby. In the process of life there are different stages we must complete in order to fully develop and mature.

My daughter was in 1st grade when she learned to spell the word "metamorphosis." I can still remember the pride in her eyes and the big smile on her face. She had accomplished something major by spelling this big word correctly and telling me what it meant. I think my smile was bigger than hers that day.

Metamorphosis describes the changes a caterpillar must go through before becoming a butterfly. During this development it enters a cocoon and remains there until its wings are fully formed. If something interrupts this process, the caterpillar leaves the cocoon unable to fly.

We also have stages in life that are critical to our development. When we skip them, it can damage our development and potential for growth.

Just like the caterpillar, it leaves us unprepared and unable to soar to new heights. Change is guaranteed to happen whether we want it to or not. So, while it is easy to remain comfortable with what's familiar, it is not always practical. When you allow yourself some flexibility to accept change and learn new things it helps make life less stressful.

I remember growing up with a Michigan Bell telephone in the house. That telephone looked and worked completely different from the telephone used today. It has a rotary dialer with numbers and letters. Similar to the "Wheel of Fortune," the caller would have to spin the wheel for each number dialed I order to compete the phone call. You had to wait for the dial wheel to turn from right, back to left, before dialing another number. That was the process in order to make a call. There was no skipping around dialing. If you were really in a hurry you could dial "0" for the operator, and then ask someone to put your call through.

Before the invention of push button phones and cell phones, it simply took longer to make phone calls. Advancements to science and technology have helped to make things more efficient and less time consuming which is a good thing, but there is also a downside when we lose our perspective and our way.

There I a sense of urgency now to everything and it affects how we treat people. Treating people with kindness and respect shouldn't get lost in the pursuit of our dreams and happiness. One of the most basic and powerful principles Jesus taught us was to love our brothers as we love ourselves. That means we should respect others and treat them the way we want to be treated. If we lose sight of this in our mad rush to get things done, then it is time to step back and reevaluate. What would Jesus do? Am I setting the type of example that He would approve of?

At an early stage in life we introduce our children to education through preparation and training. It usually takes a minimum of twelve years to complete high school; not including the time spent in day care or preschool. Sometimes students decide to drop out before completing this process. Whether it is discouragement, impatience or some other reason beyond your control, "dropping out" of school early can negatively affect your future.

Studies have shown that there is a connection between a person's education and higher wages. Better paying jobs usually require you to have obtained a certain level of education and/or training before they will consider hiring you. So, that is an incentive to remain in school and complete your education.

It is easy for someone to think that the grass is greener on the other side. That's because when you look at grass from a distance, it actual does look green and healthy. Looks can be deceiving though. When you get closer4 to take a good look, you may find that it looks completely different. Now you notice brown thin patches in the grass, perhaps some crabgrass too.

Sometimes what seems like a good idea, isn't. when you are making important decisions in your life, be informed. Make sure you have all the facts needed to make a good decision. This will allow you to weigh your option carefully and gain an understanding of that the consequences are. Let's see how this works.

DON'T SKIP THE PROCESS

A student decides to skip class one day believing that it is "no big deal." The student gets marked absent from the class, but is able to make up the work she missed. She starts to lose interest in school and begins skipping even more classes. This soon spirals out of control and the student finds herself without enough credit hours to graduate. She has to attend summer school to complete the additional credit hours needed or consider taking and passing a GED exam. This student derailed her education and career goals by not remaining focused.

Dropping out of high school can really limit your options, making it difficult to find a job, enter the military or even start your own business. It can also increase the likelihood that you will have negative contact with the criminal justice system by getting influenced or "caught up" in illegal activities. Most of us are familiar with the criminal justice system because there are so many

DON'T SKIP THE PROCESS

television shows which describe the process; a person is arrested, they may or may not be told their Miranda rights by the television officer. At some point that person asks to speak with his or her attorney. Before long, the suspect is sitting in a courtroom full of jurors. After the attorneys have each presented their case they make closing arguments and wait for the jury's decision. In most Law and Order episodes, the jury usually comes back with a guilty verdict. Next, we see the defendant being sentenced by the judge and leaving the courtroom to begin his prison sentence.

This is not to make light of the process, but to point out how familiar we have become with the steps in this process. Unlike the actors and actresses in those television scenes, real people caught in the process don't get to go home. On a daily basis there are real victims and real families torn apart on both sides.

DON'T SKIP THE PROCESS

Prisons are filled with people of all ages who made poor choices and jeopardized their future. Give yourself a chance at every opportunity to be successful by not skipping or abandoning things (such as education) that are crucial to your development.

For any student who may be struggling in school, don't be afraid or ashamed to ask for help. Recognize that sometimes you are going to have to spend more time studying, especially if it is a difficult subject for you. There are so many resources available to help you become a successful student. You have to believe in yourself and your abilities to make it happen.

Early on, my mother taught me and my sisters and brothers about the importance of church. She taught me about Jesus Christ and the Bible and its purpose. After believing and accepting Jesus Christ as my Lord and Savior I knew that I had a strong foundation to help guide me through life. I was a child then. As an adult I still rely on my Christian upbringing and the strong foundation of Jesus Christ that my mother laid the groundwork for.

Is your foundation solid? Assess your situation and your relationship with God. If you don't have one then isn't it time you developed one? Can you withstand some strong winds or trials when they come your way or are you ready to crumble in defeat? Nothing will remain standing for long without a good strong solid foundation supporting it.

You start with a position of strength in everything you do by accepting Jesus Christ as your Lord and Savior. His presence in your life will provide guidance and help you to make better decisions, no matter what situation you find yourself in.

DON'T SKIP THE PROCESS

Now, you're probably thinking, Christians make poor choices too. It's true, and the Bible is filled with stories of good Christians making bad decisions. The difference is that Christians find themselves in a far better position to recover from bad choices, especially when God has their back. When you fall down, you don't

have to stay there. God knows His children are not perfect, but he still loves us and wants what is best for us.

When we sin we also face consequences, God wants u to repent for the things we have done wrong and to ask for forgiveness. We shouldn't confuse asking for forgiveness with being given a free pass to continue committing the same sins over and over again. If you're truly committed to getting things in order and overcoming what troubles you; then you need Jesus in your life to make things right.

Romans 6:23 KJV

For the wages of sin is death, but the gift of God is eternal life through Jesus Christ our Lord.

Ephesians 6:10-11 KJV

Finally, my brethren, be strong in the Lord, and in the power of his might. Put on the whole armor of God that ye may be able to stand against the wiles of the devil.

Galatians 5:17 NIV

For the flesh desires what is contrary to the Spirit, and the Spirit what is contrary to the flesh. They are in conflict with each other so that you are not to do whatever you want.

DON'T SKIP THE PROCESS

We just read from the scripture that there is this constant internal conflict with what we want physically and spiritually. It works to keep us from being too impulsive in our decision making. It sounds a lot like our conscious; the battle between the spiritual and the

physical. Each is in direct contrast to the other and highlights the importance of having balance in our lives.

I'm sure you have seen this image before either on television or in photos. There is a person standing with a tiny angel perched on one shoulder and a tiny devil perched on the opposite shoulder. This person has a decision to make, and is caught in the middle as the angel and devil both try to persuade him to their way of thinking. It is a balancing act. If you were to always give into your physical urges without thought to how if affected other people then you would lose your humanity. You also can't become so consumed with your spiritual growth that you neglect your physical needs. Fasting is one of the most powerful ways to

strengthen your prayer life and relationship with God. Yet, we know that our bodies are only designed to go without food for so long, or we will die from starvation.

As you might expect, everything requires "balance" to keep things from getting out of control. If you spent all your time watching television and on entertainment then you would miss out on other things in your life that are more important. You may begin to neglect friends and family that need your attention.

Even your relationship with God suffers because you become too busy for Him and tune him out. This is never a good idea because God always finds a way to get out attention. So, be careful how you invest your time because once it's gone you can never get it back.

DON'T SKIP THE PROCESS

At lot of people find themselves constantly thrown into bad relationships and wonder why. It could be that they continue to make the same mistakes over and over in their selection process. If you find yourself doing something that doesn't work for you then maybe it's time to try something different.

Physical attraction to a person is one of the oldest and strongest urges known to mankind. You may meet a person and the chemistry is there. Soon your attraction turns to lust and before you know it you are in a sexual relationship. Wait a minute, for some *"relationship"* is too strong a word. You gave in to your urges and had sex. Now you're wondering why that person isn't calling you anymore. For some people this scenario plays over and over again. Never mistake lust for love. Is it possible that physical attraction can develop into something more than just sex? That depends on you and the person you're with. Relationships also require a strong foundation in order to be successful. You need to focus your attention on more than just how a person make you feel. In other words, look at the complete package a person offers, not just one aspect.

Employers interview candidates to find out if they are the right fit for a company. They make their decisions on whether or not to hire candidates based on how well they answer questions and perform tests. Just like the interviewer, it is in your best interest to learn as much as you can about your love interest. Then you can determine what your chances are for a long term relationship. What does the person do for a living? How do they act around their family and your family? Are they Saved? When they speak to you, are they quicker to support you or would they rather make you doubt yourself or humiliate you? These are questions only you can answer, but not skipping the process will prevent you from making the same mistakes over and over.

What if you're the problem? Maybe you keep missing Mr. Right or Ms. Right because no one can quite measure up to your standards. Now what if your standards are so high that even the Pope or Mother Theresa wouldn't qualify under those conditions? You get the point? Maybe you're the one standing in the way of your own happiness. In order to be successful you must have realistic standards and expectations. If your goal is to marry a billionaire, you have already eliminated more than half of the qualified pool to choose from. Attempting to build relationships simply for material possessions is a mistake. Don't let the thought of short term benefits get you "caught up" in long term regrets.

DON'T SKIP THE PROCESS

The best relationships are built on love, trust and commitment. When you find these qualities in a person,

it can inspire and support you to soar higher than you ever have.

Sometimes we rush into situations and make poor decisions because we feel we are running out of time or we want to prove something to others.

Don't be so blinded by desire or love, or the thought of marriage that you ignore the warning signs. You have the power to stop letting bad decisions ruin your life and your prospects for happiness. A person's behavior around you and others is a good indicator of what he or she is really like. If you ignore the red flags or signs that alert you to potential problems, then you may be setting yourself up for an "abusive relationship." These unhealthy relationships can quickly become dangerous or deadly. It's not worth skipping the process of learning more about a person before you get seriously involved. Remain focused on what's important and have patience so that you don't become a patient.

A young man named David approached me one day and asked me to speak with him. I didn't personally know David, but I knew was troubled and needed someone to speak with. I could see the tears standing in his eyes. It felt like pulling teeth to get David to open up about what was really bothering him, but he finally did. David explained how he messed things up with his wife of eight years because of infidelity. His wife had moved out of the house once she found out about the affair. He was so upset that he said he even considered suicide. I asked David if he and his wife still communicated, and he said, "very little." I learned that

DON'T SKIP THE PROCESS

David and his wife had separated, so I asked him to talk about the process that led up to him and his wife getting married.

I explained to him that the same things and process which lead him to his wife would be needed now to save his marriage.

Despite David's mistake, his wife needed to be reminded of why she married him, if there was any hope of salvaging their relationship. I told him to remember his vows and the many years of marriage he had experienced with his wife. David had not only violated his vows to his wife, but also her trust, and his commitment to honor her.

After some reflection, David said he still loved his wife and wanted his marriage to work. I told David he had to go back through the process of trying to regain his wife's trust because he hurt her. He knew that this would take some time and that it also depended on what his wife wanted.

That momentary decision to cheat on his wife, nearly cost David a marriage he clearly valued and cherished enough to want to save.

I saw David a few months later and he was in better spirits. David's wife has also decided to try and make their marriage work. Remember, it takes two to make a relationship work, even when there are problems. If you treat your spouse with respect and love, and in a manner that you would like to be treated, then you have a good chance at making the marriage work. Strong marriages include a healthy relationship with God as the key ingredient to their success.

Ephesians 1:19 (AMP)

So you can know and understand; what is the immeasurable, unlimited and surpassing greatness of his "God" power in and for us who believe.

1 Corinthians 13:4-7 (NIV)

Love is patient, love is kind. Its does not envy, it does not boast, it is not proud. It does not dishonor others, it is not self-seeking, it is not easily angered, it keeps no record or wrongs. Love does not delight in evil but rejoices with the truth. It always protects, always trusts, always hopes, always perseveres.

Romans 8:28 (NIV)

And we know that in all things God works for the good of those who love him, who have been called according to his purpose.

DON'T SKIP THE PROCESS

What Process am I Going Through Right Now?

_____

_____

_____

_____

_____

Identify 3-5 goals that will help complete this process.

1._____

2._____

3._____

4._____

5._____

What steps will I take to achieve my goals?

_____

_____

_____

_____

_____

How can I change my challenges into opportunities?

_____

_____

_____

_____

_____

FROM AN OFFICER'S PERSPECTIVE

2

As I reflect back into the days as a cop in the City of Detroit, I recall how dangerous and challenging the job could be. There was no limit to the types of police runs Dispatch would send me and other officers to. Crimes ranged in nature from domestic violence, homicides, kidnapping, rapes, burglaries, home invasions, robberies and drug activity. On any given day I knew I could be faced with some type of evil situation on the streets that required my attention. Many crimes were being committed by the same people over and over again. It seemed like the only thing that changed was the day and time. Some crimes were so violent and senseless that it brought out raw emotions of wanting to take matters into my own hands. If I had given into those emotions, it would have completely violated the Police Department's Code of Ethics. It also would have violated my own personal convictions and beliefs.

Romans 12:21 (KJV)

Be not overcome of evil, but overcome evil with good.

As the scripture above states, you can't overcome evil by becoming evil yourself. You overcome evil and bad acts with good ones.

A police officer's job is to apply the law equally and fairly. You can't do that if you let your personal feelings towards criminals affect your ability to do that. Police officers are held to a higher standard for good reason.

DON'T SKIP THE PROCESS

Citizens and the community want to feel protected and served by the police community, not preyed upon by it. I have found that building good relationships with the community is one of the greatest tools a police officer and the Police Department can have in being effective. Members of the community don't want to be afraid of the criminals or the police officers sworn to protect and serve them.

As always, remember, police officers are just one part in the process of the criminal justice system. It is not up to the police officer to act as judge and jury, and pass sentence on anyone. There is a court system that handles that part of the process.

I began my career with the Detroit Police Department in 1989. It was a great accomplishment for me because it was something that I had aspired to do for a long time. As a teenager, I participated in a summer youth program with the Detroit Police Department. One of my mentors was Commander McDouglas. He represented everything that I admired about being a police officer. He wore his uniform with pride and treated everyone with dignity and respect. I knew that he could be no nonsense when it came to dealing with criminals. This man was also deeply committed to giving back to the community. By investing time in the development of young people and their dreams, he was helping to improve their situations and the community. I knew I wanted to be a good police officer and have a similar impact in the lives of others. Now that I knew what I wanted, I had to put things in motion to make that dream a reality.

Let me tell you, the road to becoming a police officer was a lengthy process. After completing the employment application and passing a background check, I still had written exams and physical exams to pass. It was a grueling process. There were so many laws to learn, from traffic laws, to code of ethic laws, to criminal laws and criminal procedures. There were also countless other State laws, City municipal laws and Federal laws that I had to learn.

It was the first time I had ever studied for anything at such an advanced level or intensity, but it was absolutely necessary if I was going to be successful. Some of the material was so complex that studying on my own wasn't an option. I began joining study groups to help bolster my knowledge of the subject. I knew the only way I could pass the written exam was if I knew the laws well enough to apply it on the exam.

In addition, the police academy put its officers through a regimented physical routine that would have put PX90 to shame. The intensity of the training left us all many pounds lighter that when we first entered the academy. As you can guess, my social life with my fiancé was virtually non-existent at the time. She knew this was important to me and was supportive of my efforts. All the hard work paid off and I successfully graduated as a commissioned officer of the Detroit Police Department.

At that time, police officer's shifts rotated every 28 days. I would start working on a midnight shift, and 28 days later begin an afternoon shift, followed by a day shift 28 days later. As you can imagine, this type of work rotation wreaked havoc on an officer's ability to get any sleep. It was especially hard it you had to go straight to court after just finishing your shift. The sleep problems associated with this practice had a negative effect on police officer's performances, such as   tickets with inaccurate or illegible information. Some reports were so poorly written that prosecutors couldn't understand what the officers were saying and had to dismiss the cases. There was no doubt this long term practice was taking a toll on officers and negatively affecting their performances. It would be years later, but thankfully, the Mayor and Police Department chose to end this practice.

I brought this up because sometimes there are steps in a process that may have worked welled at one time but no longer do. Whether you own a company or work for someone else, there are times when changes are necessary to keep operating effectively.

Being a cop is a profession that a lot of people may want, but it is not for everyone. Police officers not only serve and protect the community, they should help build it up with their presence. You will deal with people from all walks of life and every race and ethnicity as you do your job. Your social skills and how you communicate with others is just as important as your knowledge of the law.

DON'T SKIP THE PROCESS

Officers who rely too heavily or improperly on force are abusing their positions of authority. When this happens they risk being brought up on charges and convicted of crimes themselves. In effect, they turn out to be no better than the criminals they once chased.

Law enforcement is always in need of good men and women with strong character and integrity.

If a career in law enforcement interest you, begin by asking yourself tough questions.

Am I interested in this career for the right reasons or selfish ones? Can I work well with people? Do I handle stressful situations well? These are just a few of the many questions you should be asking yourself. Don't skip the process of evaluating your personal traits with the requirements needed to be a police officer before making a commitment.

FROM AN OFFICER'S PERSPECTIVE

_____

_____

_____

_____

_____

_____

_____

_____

_____

_____

_____

_____

_____

FROM AN OFFICER'S PERSPECTIVE

_____

_____

_____

_____

_____

_____

_____

_____

_____

_____

_____

_____

_____

_____

_____

_____

SPIRITUAL ASSURANCE

3

1 Peter 4:10-11 (NIV)

Each of you should use whatever gift you have received to serve others, as faithful stewards of God's grace in its various forms. [11]If anyone speaks, they should do so as one who speaks the very words of God. If anyone serves, they should do so with the strength God provides, so that in all things God may be praised through Jesus

Christ. To him be the glory and the power for ever and ever. Amen.

Acts 18:9-11 (NIV)

One night the Lord spoke to Paul in a vision: "Do not be afraid; keep on speaking, do not be silent. For I am with you, and no one is going to attack and harm you, because I have many people in this city." Paul stayed for a year and a half, teaching them the word of God.

Ephesians 6:12 (KJV)

For we wrestle not against flesh and blood, but against principalities, against powers, against the rulers of the darkness of this world, against spiritual wickedness in high places.

DON'T SKIP THE PROCESS

There are times in life when we face odds and challenges that seem almost impossible to overcome. No matter what goals we set to achieve our objective, we know that it is going to be an uphill struggle all the way. That's because sometimes the problem is bigger than us. At times like this we have to remember that the battle isn't ours, it's the Lord's to fight. Dr. Martin Luther King is a great example for the point I am making here. He knew that he faced tremendous obstacles in trying to end years of institutional racism and discrimination. Some of his fellow preachers even tried to discourage him, but Dr. King didn't waver from his message of non-violent protest. Dr. King remained steadfast in his faith and commitment to end Jim Crow laws. Although his protests were peaceful, those who opposed his views still reacted with violence. Dr. King may have been discouraged at times, but he wasn't deterred. He kept marching and believing in God that his vision to end racial segregation in the country could be achieved.

It is hard to imagine the personal toll Dr. King's work had on him and his family. This humble preacher who preached non-violence was physically attacked, had his home bombed several times, was arrested an d placed in jail more than 25 times. He also received numerous death threats.

If we're honest with ourselves, there aren't too many of us who would have sacrificed so much. Dr. King knew this battle was bigger than him, and that it would require supernatural power. Thanks to his effects (and many people who supported him) we saw the end of racial segregation, and the creation of civil rights laws.

When Dr. King gave his "I Have a Dream," speech, he spoke of a world that would not judge his children by the color of their skin. He knew that the road to get there was a long and difficult one, but his faith in God and perseverance helped save the nation. We can continue Dr. King's legacy and good work by staying the course and continuing to fight for righteousness.

Just like Dr. King, we need spiritual assurances from God. We need to read our Bibles daily and study the Word for ourselves, not just be told what is in the Bible. The Bible is a weapon and it prepares us for battle. Many of the problems we see in the world are actually the result of spiritual warfare meant to destroy us.

John 1:1 (KJV)

In the beginning was the Word, and the Word was with God, and the Word was God.

DON'T SKIP THE PROCESS

In order to win these battles we have to be prepared by being knowledgeable of God's Word and remaining prayerful and faithful that He will deliver us. Reading and studying God's Word, again, reminds us that we are not alone and that nothing is impossible with him.

When you have a vision or are really passionate about something, people may try to discourage you or make you doubt yourself. You have to determine if the person doing this is well intentioned and doing if for your good, or if it is meant to keep you from being successful.

People who really care about you try to support you whenever possible, even with constructive criticism, they try build you up, not mislead you or tear you down. If you have friends or family members who are always negative and never offer anything positive then you need to limit your time around them because you will always doubt yourself and your ability to be successful in life.

Ephesians 4:29 (NIV)

Do not let any unwholesome talk come out of your mouths, but only what is helpful for building others up according to their needs, that it may benefit those who listen.

Les Brown once said, "The best revenge is a massive success." There will *always* be someone who doubts you or tries to discourage you from achieving your goals. Don't let this person or people like this have the final say on your destiny. Focus your energy on staying on course and let your success speak for itself. Let no one knock you out of your squares, step out when you get ready.

DON'T SKIP THE PROCESS

In order to be successful you have to set goals and work towards achieving those goals. It is important to have positive role models and people who speak positively and support you in your endeavors. Why would you want to waste your time and energy on negativity or anyone who fosters that type of environment? It will not only frustrate you, it will prevent you from accomplishing your goals in life.

When Dr. Martin Luther King Jr. wrote the famous "Letter from the Birmingham Jail," he stated, "time is neutral, it can be used either destructively or constructively." That statement is so true; it is up to you how you choose to use your time.

Are you making the best investment of your time by learning as much as you can about things that are important to you? What about your investment of time with the company that you keep? Are they helping you

DON'T SKIP THE PROCESS

to grow or are they stunting your growth? Only you can answer these questions.

I pose these two questions for your thought.

Who are you leading and for what purpose? Is it for your own glorification or is it for God's glorification? We have far too many leaders who are misleading others for their own personal gain, instead of trying to help others.

Today we may be marching to a different beat than that of yesterday, but we must still stay focused. The march for peace, justice, equality and better quality of life for all people (not just some) must continue. We all have something to contribute to this process; in our homes, neighborhoods and communities. Let us not skip the process of showing leadership and a desire to help others.

I was driving my youngest daughter to her dance class in the middle of a snow storm. The windshield began to get covered with snow and salt from the roadways. We could see cars directly in front of us as their tires began spinning and kicking up snow and salt from the pavement. It was typical Michigan weather for winter, but that didn't make it any less dangerous. We were traveling on the freeway with other cars and I was unable to pull over to the shoulder. I knew my daughter was anxious. I didn't want her to worry, so I began talking to her as I continued to drive.

I explained that I had to keep driving and moving the car forward (with caution) although my vision was impaired by the blowing snow covering my windshield. Even as my wiper blades swung back and forth at the highest possible setting, it was still difficult to see.

My vision became even worse as the wiper blades smeared a mixture of snow and salt across the windshield. It looked like one big chalkboard that hadn't been erased in weeks. I hit the button to release windshield wiper fluid because visibility was really bad at this point. I was relieved to see the blue spray shooting up in streams. Squirting the windshield with the spray worked. It cleared my vision and gave me a better view of the road and what lay ahead.

Just like that snow covered windshield we sometimes become overwhelmed by what's going on in our lives. When that happens it clouds our thinking and ability to see a way out of our troubles. No matter what road you're on, remember to let God navigate your path. When you have faith in Him, he makes all things clear.

Let us also encourage our young people by helping them to reach their potential. It is okay to dream and make plans to pursue those dreams. Anything is achievable if you put your mind and heart into it and remain focused. Teaching young people how to be confident in themselves and their abilities will help them to take pride in their appearance and their work. Let's also teach our young people to love and respect themselves. When we support our young people and invest a positive influence in their lives it empowers them to reach their fullest potential in life.

Some people make excuses that they can't do any better because of the environment around them. That doesn't have to always be the case. Steer clear of negative people and situations. I cannot stress this enough. Change your environment if you can.

Sometimes what you consider a roadblock I actually something that is good for you. Roadblocks are sometimes necessary to slow us down and prevent us from following the wrong crowd or going down the wrong path to destruction.

I believe one of the gifts God has blessed me with is my ability to listen and communicate with other people. At least once or twice a week someone comes to me seeking advice or just because they need someone who will listen to them and their situation. I know God is directing them for such as time as this and I have to be ready at all times to do God's will.

There are people in your lives right ow who may just need you to listen and offer support as they work through a difficult situation. Whether you are at home, work, school or church, you should find time to help others and offer them support.

Are you ready to accept the assignments God has for you?

Your life story should reflect the positive impact you have had in leading others towards salvation and the Kingdom of God. You have the potential to be a positive influence in your home, workplace, church and communities by the good works that you perform.

DON'T SKIP THE PROCESS

Commit yourself to becoming a positive influence and

help uplift others that you meet along the way.

SPIRITUAL ASSURANCES

SPIRITUAL ASSURANCES

_____

_____

_____

_____

_____

_____

_____

_____

_____

_____

_____

_____

_____

_____

_____

_____

_____

_____

INSTRUCTIONS

4

My wife loves buying furniture or equipment that must be assembled. She know that I really don't like putting things together. There always seems to be some missing parts or screws, or some hole that wasn't quite drilled properly or at all. Although my wife knows I don't like putting things together she continues to buy them. Sometimes she says she will assemble it herself, but somehow the job still ends up with me doing all the work. I have know her long enough to know this isn't some type of torture meant to wear me down. She usually thinks she has gotten a bargain and the assembly necessary is a small price to pay for the deal.

I usually begin the process by looking at a photo of what the finished project should look like. Then I pull all the pieces out of the box and quickly toss the instructions aside. After I have recovered from looking at all the pieces that look like they belong to a 1001 piece jigsaw puzzle, I begin to work. At some point my wife asks me the question she repeatedly asks again and again in this type of situation, "Why don't you like reading the instructions?" I assure her I don't need the instructions to finish the project. After all, it isn't rocket science. As if I am performing surgery, I begin to drill here and turn a screw there; trying to find a home for all those screws and pieces scattered on the floor.

Before I am done, I have worked up a sweat that any Olympic runner would be proud of. Then I notice that

DON'T SKIP THE PROCESS

there are still too many pieces and screws that haven't been used. Something about the finished project doesn't seem right either. I soon realize that something important has been left out of the assembly process. I have to detach and unscrew everything and start all over; this time using the instructions for guidance.

Guess what? If I hadn't skipped the process of reading the instructions, I could have saved myself a lot of time and energy. I'm sure more than a few of you can relate to this situation. You think that looking at the picture on the outside of the box is sufficient, or you're in a hurry to finish.

I chose to skip the process of reading instructions because I thought it wasn't necessary and wanted a short cut to finishing the project.

Instructions must be pretty important. It is one of the few

things you find that is consistently written in different languages, no matter what the product is.

In life, instructions come in many forms. It could be house rules that you have to create to keep order in your household. It could be the employee handbook or policies and procedures at work. Failure to know and follow these instructions could result in discipline or worse, losing your job.

Unless you are familiar with a process, it may not be wise to skip the instructions. Keep in mind that even when you're familiar with the rules, they can still change. That is why you will find employers and schools constantly updating policies and procedures as laws change and new issues arise; and providing training.

Before you decide to skip a step in any process, make sure it is one that you can afford to skip. Some steps are just too important to skip and can cause more harm than good.

I know that I'm on an assignment from God. I am being used as an instrument on this side of Heaven to encourage, enlighten, instill, impart, and enrich the lives of those seeking help. It started before I was a teenager, people seemed to gravitate towards me for conversation. It didn't matter if it was friends or family members, even complete strangers would ask me to speak with them about their problems.

People seemed to know that I would listen, offer good advice and not abuse their trust. I know this was no coincidence. I believe God was directing them towards me so that He could use me to deliver the message they needed to hear. I don't take this 'gift' from God lightly. I have an obligation to use it responsibly. Whenever I'm approached by anyone seeking help, I always ask the Lord for guidance and the words to speak therefore, giving them confirmation from God. It lets them know only God knows their problems and has used me to speak these things out to them. God is omnipotent *(all powerful)* and omniscient *(all knowing)*. I know it is only Him working through me, and allowing me to use my gift to be a blessing to others. I have been doing this for over thirty-five years. When God is using you to fulfill His purpose, you don't want to skip the assignment. It is just too important. We have to re-tool our own thinking process from one of negativity to one of positivity.

Someone might think it's alright to skip a step in the process because it's not necessary. Even if you make this determination it should be based on you knowing all the facts and making an informed decision. Planning is an important step in starting and completing whatever goals you set for yourself.

DON'T SKIP THE PROCESS

Life is a process we must all go through. Each and every day, we make decisions that significantly affect us. Sometimes we give very little thought to these decisions and the impact they will have.

If you are in a position to keep someone from making a mistake, then you should be a positive influence. Sometimes sharing your own personal experiences and the outcome is the best instruction manual around because it provides guidance. Remember, God blesses us to that we can be a blessing to others!

John 14:26 (KJV)

But the Comforter, which is the Holy Ghost, whom the Father will send in my name, he shall teach you all things, and bring all things to your remembrance, whatsoever I have said unto you.

DON'T SKIP THE PROCESS

The Father, Son and Holy Ghost *(The Trinity)* in ALL things, makes His instructions plain. He reminds us that He would not leave us alone, to fend for ourselves, that we only need to call on him for direction in our journey to becoming successful in life as well as being a saint in His Kingdom.

DON'T SKIP THE PROCESS

Instructions

_____

_____

_____

_____

_____

_____

_____

_____

_____

_____

_____

_____

_____

_____

_____

_____

Instructions

_____

_____

_____

_____

_____

_____

_____

_____

_____

_____

_____

_____

_____

_____

_____

_____

WHEN IN DOUBT, CHECK IT OUT

Scriptural Guidance in Times of Trouble

5

The best way to gain an understanding of the Bible and how it applies to your life is by reading it and meditating on the scriptures. You can find wisdom and guidance within it's pages for whatever troubles you.

Psalm 119: 105 (NKJV)

Your word is a lamp to my feet and a light to my path.

DON'T SKIP THE PROCESS

Below you will find some ten (10) different sets of scriptures to study and pray, at least once a day over the course of (10) days. I believe each set of scriptures has a message which will help you and provide you with a clearer understanding of how the scriptures applies to your life. Use them as guidance in your daily experiences and as a spiritual weapon to strengthen you when facing whatever challenges come your way. The scriptures and messages attached can be found in your Bible or if you're on-line you can use www.biblegateway.com

If you keep your mind stayed on Jesus Christ without skipping the process of studying His Word, you will be on your way to staying focused and ground in everything that you do.

1. STRENGTH

Isaiah 40:31 (KJV)

But they that wait upon the lord shall renew strength. They shall mount up with wings like eagles; they shall run and not be weary; they shall walk and not faint.

1 Corinthians 10:13 (KJV)

There hath no temptation taken you but such as is common to man: but God is faithful, who will not suffer you to be tempted above that ye are able; but will with the temptation also make a way to escape, that ye may be able to bear it.

Isaiah 41:10 (KJV)

Fear thou not; for I am with thee: be not dismayed; for I am thy God: I will strengthen thee; yea, I will help thee; yea, I will uphold thee with the right hand of my righteousness.

DON'T SKIP THE PROCESS

1 Chronicles 16:11 (NIV)

Look to the LORD and his strength; seek his face always.

THE MESSAGE:

Why would you ever complain, O Jacob, or whine, Israel, saying, "God has lost track of me. He doesn't care what happens to me?" Don't you know anything? Haven't you been listening? God doesn't come and go. God lasts. He's Creator of all you can see or imagine. He doesn't get tired out, doesn't pause to catch his breath. And he knows everything, inside and out. He energizes those who get tired, gives fresh strength to dropouts. For even young people tire and drop out, young folk in their prime stumble and fall. But those who wait upon God get fresh strength. The spread their wings and soar like eagles. They run and don't get tired, they walk and don't lag behind.

1. Daily Thoughts to be Prayed Over

_____

_____

_____

_____

_____

_____

_____

_____

_____

_____

_____

_____

_____

_____

_____

2. SALVATION

John 14:16 (NIV)

Jesus answered, "I am the way and the truth and the life. No one comes to the Father except through me.

Romans 10:9 (KJV)

That if thou shalt confess with thy mouth the Lord Jesus, and shalt believe in thine heart that God hath raised him from the dead, thou shalt be saved.

Philippians 2:10-11 (NIV)

That at the name of Jesus every knee should bow, in heaven and on earth and under the earth, [11]and every tongue acknowledge that Jesus Christ is LORD, to the glory of God the Father.

John 3:16-17 (NIV)

For God so loved the world that he gave his one and only Son, that whoever believes in him shall not perish but have eternal life. For God did not send his Son into the world to condemn the world, but to save the world through him.

THE MESSAGE:

You're blessed when you stay on course, walking steadily on the road revealed by God. You're blessed when you follow his directions, doing your best to find him. That's right, you don't have to go off on your own; you walk straight along the road he set. You, God, prescribed the right way to live; now you expect us to live it. Oh, that my steps might be steady, keeping to the course you set. Then I'd never have any regrets in comparing my life with your counsel. I thank you speaking straight from your heart; I learned the pattern of your righteous ways. I'm going to do what you tell me to do; don't ever walk off and leave me.

2. Daily Thoughts to be Prayed Over

_____

_____

_____

_____

_____

_____

_____

_____

_____

_____

_____

_____

_____

_____

_____

3. REMAINING GROUNDED

Proverbs 16:3 (KJV)

Commit thy works unto the lord, and thy thoughts shall be established.

Proverbs 16:3 (KJV)

Roll your works upon the Lord [commit and trust them wholly to Him; He will cause your thoughts to become agreeable to His will, and] so shall your plans be established and succeed.

Mark 10:45 (KJV)

For even the Son of man came not to be ministered unto, but to minister, and to give his life a ransom for many.

DON'T SKIP THE PROCESS

Philippians 2:5-7 (NIV)

In your relationships with one another, have the same mindset as Christ Jesus: Who, being in very nature[a] God, did not consider equality with God something to be used to his own advantage; rather, he made himself nothing by taking the very nature of a servant, being made in human likeness.

2 chronicles 7:14 (KJV)

If my people, which are called by my name, shall humble themselves, and pray, and seek my face, and turn from their wicked ways; then will I hear from heaven, and will forgive their sin, and will heal their land.

THE MESSAGE:

God does not show preference to people based on the positions they hold in society or the amount of wealth they have. We are all privileged to be His children; and in His eyes we are all equal. Jesus brought the gospel to anyone who would listen; the sick and poor, even those who shunned by society. Surely, we can follow His example in our own lives, spreading the gospel and message of inclusion in a world that desperately needs it.

3. Thoughts of the day to be prayed over

_____

_____

_____

_____

_____

_____

_____

_____

_____

_____

_____

_____

_____

_____

_____

_____

4. SAME MINDED SAINTS/PRAYER WARRIORS

Matthew 18:20 (KJV)

For where two or three are gathered together in my name, there am I in the midst of them.

James 5:16 (KJV)

Confess your faults one to another, and pray one for another, that ye may be healed. The effectual fervent prayer of a righteous man availeth much.

1 CORINTHIANS 1:4 (ESV)

I give thanks to my God always for you because of the grace of God that was given you in Christ Jesus…

1 Thessalonians 5:16-18 (KJV)

Rejoice evermore. Pray without ceasing. In everything give thanks: for this is the will of God in Christ Jesus concerning you.

THE MESSAGE:

"Take this most seriously: A yes on earth is yes in heaven; a no on earth is a no in heaven. What you say to one another is eternal. I mean this. When two of you get together on anything at all on earth and make a prayer of it, my Father in heaven goes into action. And then two or three of you are together because of me, you can be sure that I'll be there."

4. Thoughts of the day to be prayed over

_____

_____

_____

_____

_____

_____

_____

_____

_____

_____

_____

_____

_____

_____

_____

5. ENCOURAGEMENT

Philippians 4:13 (KJV)

I can do all things through Christ which strengthened me.

PROVERBS 3:5-6 (KJV)

Trust in the LORD with all thine heart; and lean not unto thine own understanding. In all thy ways acknowledge him, and he shall direct thy paths.

PROVERBS 18-10 (KJV)

The name of the LORD is a strong tower: the righteous runneth into it, and is safe.

JOHN 16:33 KJV

These things I have spoken unto you, that in me ye might have peace. In the world ye shall have tribulation: but be of good cheer; I have overcome the world.

PSALM 46:1-3 (NIV)

God is our refuge and strength, an ever-

present help in trouble. Therefore we will not

fear, though the earth give way and the mountains

fall into the heart of the sea, though its waters roar and

foam and the mountains quake with their surging.

"Selah'"

THE MESSAGE:

I'm glad in God, far happier than you would ever guess—happy that you're again showing such strong concern for me. Not that you ever quit praying and thinking about me. You just had no chance to show it. Actually, I don't have a sense of needing anything personally. I've learned by now to be quite content whatever my circumstances. I'm just as happy being an humble servant of Christ telling his message for us. I've found the recipe for being happy whether full or hungry, hands full or empty. Whatever I have, wherever I am, I can make it through anything in the One who makes me who I am. For I know I can do all things through Christ which strengthens me. It was a beautiful thing that you came along side me in my times of need and have never left me.

5. Thoughts of the Day to Be Prayed Over

_____

_____

_____

_____

_____

_____

_____

_____

_____

_____

_____

_____

_____

_____

6. REFUSING TO GIVE UP

Galatians 6:9 (KJV)

And let us not be weary in well doing, for in due season we shall reap, if we faint not.

Ephesians 2:10 (NIV)

For we are God's handiwork, created in Christ Jesus to do good works, which God prepared in advance for us to do.

Philippians 4:6-7 (NKJV)

Be anxious for nothing, but in everything by prayer and supplication, with thanksgiving, let your requests be made known to God; and the peace of God, which surpasses all understanding, will guard your hearts and minds through Christ Jesus.

DON'T SKIP THE PROCESS

Psalm 37:1-5 (KJV)

Fret not thyself because of evildoers, neither be thou envious against the workers of iniquity. For they shall soon be cut down like the grass, and wither as the green herb. Trust in the LORD, and do good; so shalt thou dwell in the land, and verily thou shalt be fed. Delight thyself also in the LORD: and he shall give thee the desires of thine heart. Commit thy way unto the LORD; trust also in him; and he shall bring it to pass.

THE MESSAGE:

So let's not allow ourselves to get fatigued doing good. At the right time we will harvest a good crop if we don't give up, or quit. Right now, therefore, every time we get the chance, let us work for the benefit of all, starting with the people closest to us in the community of faith.

6. Thoughts of the day to be prayed over

_____

_____

_____

_____

_____

_____

_____

_____

_____

_____

_____

_____

_____

_____

_____

_____

7. NEED RESCUE

2 Corinthians 1:3-4 (KJV)

Blessed be God, even the Father of our Lord Jesus Christ, the Father of mercies, and the God of all comfort; Who comforteth us in all our tribulation, that we may be able to comfort them which are in any trouble, by the comfort wherewith we ourselves are comforted of God.

Psalm 55:22 (KJV)

Cast thy burden upon the LORD, and he shall sustain thee: he shall never suffer the righteous to be moved.

Psalm 121:1-2 (KJV)

DON'T SKIP THE PROCESS

I will lift up mine eyes unto the hills, from whence cometh my help. My help cometh from the LORD, which made heaven and earth.

Psalm 91:10 (NIV)

If you say, "The LORD is my refuge," and you make the Most High your dwelling, no harm will overtake you, no disaster will come near your tent.

THE MESSAGE:

All praise to the God and Father of our Master, Jesus the Messiah! Father of all mercy! God of all healing counsel! He comes alongside us when we go through hard times, and before you know it, he brings us alongside someone else who is going through hard times too. We can be there for that person just as God

was there for us. For we know that weeping endureth

for but a night, but joy comes in the morning.

7. Thoughts of the day to be prayed over

_____

_____

_____

_____

_____

_____

_____

_____

_____

_____

_____

_____

8. WHEN YOU NEED SELF DISCIPLINE

2 Corinthians 5:14-15 (KJV)

For the love of Christ constraineth us; because we thus judge, that if one died for all, then were all dead: And that he died for all, that they which live should not henceforth live unto themselves, but unto him which died for them, and rose again.

1 Peter 5:8 (KJV)

Be sober, be vigilant; because your adversary the devil, as a roaring lion, walketh about, seeking whom he may devour:

Galatians 5:22-23 (NIV)

But the fruit of the Spirit is love, joy, peace, forbearance, kindness, goodness, faithfulness, gentleness and self-control. Against such things there is no law.

THE MESSAGE:

That keeps us vigilant, you can be sure. It's no light thing to know that we'll all one day stand in that place of Judgment. That's why we work urgently with everyone we meet to get them ready to face God. God alone knows how well we do this, but I hope you realize how much and deeply we care. We're not saying this to make ourselves look good to you. We just thought it would make you feel good, proud even, that we're on your side and not just nice to your face as so many people are. If I acted crazy, I did it for God; if I acted overly serious, I did it for you. Christ's love has moved me to such extremes. His love has the first and last word in everything we do.

8. Thoughts of the day to be prayed over

_____

_____

_____

_____

_____

_____

_____

_____

_____

_____

_____

_____

_____

_____

_____

9. Be Anxious for Nothing

Philippians 4:6-7 KJV

Be careful for nothing; but in every thing by prayer and supplication with thanksgiving let your requests be made known to God. And the peace of God, which passeth all understanding, shall keep your hearts and minds through Christ Jesus.

Mathew 6:25-27 (NIV)

Therefore I tell you, do not worry about your life, what you will eat or drink; or about your body, what you will wear. Is not life more than food, and the body more than clothes? Look at the birds of the air; they do not sow or reap or store away in barns, and yet your heavenly Father feeds them. Are you not much more valuable than they? Can any one of you by worrying add a single hour to your life?

DON'T SKIP THE PROCESS

Hebrews 13:5-6

Keep your lives free from the love of money and be content with what you have, because God has said,

"Never will I leave you; never will I forsake you."

So we say with confidence, "The Lord is my helper; I will not be afraid. What can mere mortals do to me?

THE MESSAGE:

Don't fret or worry. Instead of worrying, pray. Let petitions and praises shape your worries into prayers, letting God know your concerns. Before you know it, a sense of God's wholeness, everything coming together for good, will come and settle you down. It's wonderful what happens when Christ displaces worry at the center of your life.

9. Thoughts of the day to be prayed over

_____

_____

_____

_____

_____

_____

_____

_____

_____

_____

_____

_____

_____

_____

_____

_____

10. GIVING GOD PRAISE

Psalm 34:1 (KJV)

I will bless the LORD at all times: his praise shall continually be in my mouth.

John 4:23-24 (NIV)

Yet a time is coming and has now come when the true worshipers will worship the Father in the Spirit and in truth, for they are the kind of worshipers the Father seeks. God is spirit, and his worshipers must worship in the Spirit and in truth."

Psalm 117:1-2 (KJV)

O praise the LORD, all ye nations: praise him, all ye people. For his merciful kindness is great toward us: and the truth of the LORD endureth forever. Praise ye the LORD.

Psalm 150:1-6 (NIV)

Praise ye the LORD. Praise God in his sanctuary: praise him in the firmament of his power. Praise him for his mighty acts: praise him according to his excellent greatness. Praise him with the sound of the trumpet: praise him with the psaltery and harp. Praise him with the timbrel and dance: praise him with stringed instruments and organs. Praise him upon the loud cymbals: praise him upon the high sounding cymbals.

Let every thing that hath breath praise the LORD. Praise ye the LORD.

THE MESSAGE:

God is an awesome God! His goodness and mercy knows no bounds. Have you thanked him today?

10. Thoughts of the Day to Be Prayed Over

_____

_____

_____

_____

_____

_____

_____

_____

_____

_____

_____

IS THE CHURCH IN YOU?

Working for a major retail organizations listed in Forbes and a Fortune 500 business comes with a lot of responsibilities. This industry relies on its employees to provide good customer service and create an inviting shopping experience which encourages customers to become loyal customers.

Success depends on putting the right people in the right positions to obtain positive results. Employee selection and training is a critical part of this process.

1 Corinthians 3:16 (KJV)

Know ye not that ye are the temple of God, and that the Spirit of God dwelleth in you?

Galatians 5:22-23 (NIV)

But the fruit of the Spirit is love, joy, peace, forbearance, kindness, goodness, faithfulness, gentleness and self-control. Against such things there is no law.

When you are constantly working with people from all walks of life on a regular basis, you will see the good, the bad and the ugly depending on what situation arises. No, I am not talking about personal appearance. I am speaking to behaviors. You may just happen to catch a demanding customer on a bad day and their disposition *(which may or may not have started with you)* places you in an awkward position. You can't control how a customer acts, but you do have control over your own reaction. Depending on how you respond, you can either make matters worse, or improve the situation. For instance, shouting and yelling at an angry customer is likely to get you disciplined or fired. It is not professional, not is it appropriate.

You also have to be mindful that employees are also people who occasionally have bad days, but still come to work and try to perform as if everything is okay. When possible, I try to lend an ear and listen to what is effecting an employee. The encouragement and support provided by just listening at times, can help get a good employee back on track.

When I interview candidates, I also try to determine if they possess the necessary skills and personality traits to be successful. Can they handle stressful situations without quickly losing their temper? Are they respectful towards others even when they disagree with them? A potential employee's disposition is just as important as the credentials which gained them the interview.

My purpose in writing this chapter is to explain the concept of church and how it operates in the lives of true believers of Christ, and also, to share how fruits of the spirit work in connection with this. Now, most of us only think of church as a physical building with a location. In actuality, our bodies are considered temples and the church is in us. What this means is that we are to learn the Word of God through reading, studying and meditating on the Bible and then applying it to the outside world. In effect, we are the church because we take what we have learned and bring it to the world for them to see.

We manifest the teachings of Christ through our actions and encounters with others. Some people may never set foot in a church building, but they are still able to witness God's grace and mercy and be lead towards a relationship with Christ through the examples you set. Fruits of the spirit are characteristics that Christians are to uphold and exemplify in their lives and the lives of others.

Christians know that they should treat everyone with respect and love. Instead of spreading rumors and instigating fights they should be trying to maintain peace in the workplace. They should also show signs of goodness, patience and self-control. In other words, when you are operating with these gifts inside you, it is reflected in the work you do. Sometimes, a Christian may still be struggling to "perfect" their gifts from the

Lord. I know that many of us have, and still face challenges with patience. If this is the case for you, don't give up on yourself. If you remain faithful, stay in the Word and apply these principles to your life you will see a change for the better.

When people see fruits of the spirit *(love, joy, peace, patience, kindness, goodness, faithfulness, gentleness, self-control)* at work in you, they are really seeing God's presence in you and in your life. How powerful a statement is that? So, no matter what position you hold or where you work, try to be a shinning example of God's goodness, grace and mercy by how you treat others.

1 Corinthians 3:16 (KJV)

Know ye not that ye are the temple of God, and that the Spirit of God dwelleth in you?

Galatians 5:22-23 (NIV)

But the fruit of the Spirit is love, joy, peace, forbearance, kindness, goodness, faithfulness, gentleness and self-control. Against such things there is no law.

IS THE CHURCH IN YOU?

_____

_____

_____

_____

_____

_____

_____

_____

_____

_____

_____

_____

_____

_____

_____

IS THE CHURCH IN YOU?

READY OR NOT, HERE I COME

7

Growing up as a child we had many of games to play to keep us occupied. Though our family was very poor, it wasn't until we were well into our teens or grown that we figured that out, for with our God fearing mother, it was a well-kept secret within herself. Our mother made sure there was never a dull moment in the household. There was always something to do. My mother made sure every neighborhood we lived in had a school playground or some recreation nearby. We would play baseball all day from sun up to sun down. We were never told, "go outside a play", because it was always second nature to us. It was the opposite for us, as we often were told to come in because it was getting dark outside.

There was this one game that we used to play where one person would close their eyes while the others would go and hide. It was called, "Hide-N-Go Seek." The person doing the counting would count to ten and then say "ready or not here I come." If you were really good at hiding you would strategically place yourself where you could still see the person counting, but avoid capture.

As I got older, I stopped playing certain foot games such as 'Hide-N-Go Seek' but continued playing my baseball, football, basketball and even a little tennis.

DON'T SKIP THE PROCESS

My mother taught us about Jesus Christ at a very young age. We learned that accepting Jesus Christ as the son of God, and believing that he died for our sins and rose again from the dead meant that we too could have salvation. Sundays were special in my household. My mother made sure there were no excuses for us to miss church service. We prepared a day in advance and our clothes were set out for the next day. Each Sunday she would take all nine of us to church where we stayed for Sunday school and 11:00 a.m. morning worship services. Sometimes we also attend afternoon service. My mother's strong influence and love wasn't wasted on us, neither was her love for the church.

We realized the importance of seeking God's presence in our lives and remaining faithful. As I matured in a man, I could see a big difference in my Christian walk and faith. My spiritual development strengthened as I turned more towards the Bible for guidance and remain prayerful. It was a process started by my mother. She knew that if she laid the right "foundation" for her children that it would remain with us even as adults.

To this day, I can still remember my mother's words to each of us, she would say, "Mama can't keep tabs on you always, so make sure no matter where you go, or who you're with when you leave this house, always remember to remain in the Lord's house." This was my mother's way of reminding us to remain true to our values and Christian upbringing; our moral compass in helping us make good Godly decisions. Even if we were outside of church walls we were to behave as if we had been raised in the church. She reminded us that we could go *(die)* at any time without warning and that we had to be ready *(Saved)*. This still holds true today. Tomorrow is not promised. Salvation and the promise of life after death comes only to those who accept Jesus Christ as their Lord and Savior.

My mother would also say, "You better hope nothing happens to you because I will not drag your butt into the church. "This was her way of reminding us that if we strayed too far from the church that we shouldn't expect a proper church funeral when we depart this world. Once again, this was mon sharing tough love and advice meant to keep us on track. She was good at doing that.

Matthew 24:42-45

Watch therefore: for ye know not what hour your Lord doth come. But know this, that if the good man of the house had known in what watch the thief would come, he would have watched, and would not have suffered his house to be broken up. Therefore be ye also ready: for in such an hour as ye think not the Son of man cometh. Who then is a faithful and wise servant, whom his lord hath made ruler over his household, to give them meat in due season?

DON'T SKIP THE PROCESS

No one knows the future or the day or the hour that Jesus will return. Unlike Hide-N-Seek, there may be no counting or warning statement that He is approaching. The only way we can be prepared is to have accepted Jesus Christ as our Lord and Savior and obtain the gift of salvation.

God does what he wants in his own time because his time is not our time. Mom remained supportive of us, even as we grew older and our careers and families took us in different directions. Mom's message was clear that it was important to be saved and have a relationship with Jesus, that was above all else. I thank God everyday that my family is saved. But it reminds me of the game we played growing up. The only difference in that game was we had a chance to prepare and hide while someone else would count and say at the end of the count, "ready or not, here I come."

DON'T SKIP THE PROCESS

You don't get that warning call from above where you can go and run and hide. You can't hide from God and sure can't out run him either. If you are not saved by his grace and have not accepted Jesus I your life, you will be caught, but not by the right one, unless you just don't care or understand.

John 10:10 (NKJV)

The thief cometh not, but for to steal, and to kill, and to destroy; I am come that they might have life, and that they have it more abundantly.

Most thieves move quickly and prefer darkness so that you can't see them in action. As they quietly move about seeing what they can steal, they often have the element of surprise working in their favor. When you accept Jesus Christ as your Savior, you are assured victory over the thief in all its forms because no weapon directed against you will work. *(Isaiah 54:17).* Isn't it better to be prepared for 'something' than to be caught off guard with nothing? "It's better to have Jesus and not need him than to need him and not have him." Don't let the, 'not need' him part fool you though. We are always in need of Jesus Christ's presence in our lives.

This quote is a reminder that tomorrow is not promised and we shouldn't wait to accept salvation at a "convenient time."

Yet, some people will wait until that very crucial moment hits them before calling on the Lord. What if you waited so long that you are now at a point where it's too late? Situations occur all the time that we have no control over. Unlike the game Hide-N-Seek, there may be no warning before we face danger or trouble. Don't wait to accept Jesu Christ. I can't express this enough. Be ready when the time does come to depart this life.

DON'T SKIP THE PROCESS

Remember, as I've previously stated, we operate on God's timing and not or own. With Jesus there is no need for turning the clock back, for our past transgressions are already forgiven. With Jesus there is only room for moving forward in life.

For sure, Hide-N-Go Seek was fun and games back in the day, but our Christian walk, the reality of Jesus is *here and now*. There really is no ready or not, because Jesus is coming. There will be no warning signal that you hear like every first of the month in case of an attack, invasion or severe weather, coming to your hometown. The only "whether" you should be concerned about is "whether" you and your loved one are saved when the trumpet sounds upon Jesus' return.

Ready or Not, Here I Come

_____
_____
_____
_____
_____
_____
_____
_____
_____
_____
_____
_____
_____
_____
_____

GOD'S PROCESS BEING USED IN ME AND THROUGH ME

8

I recall when the church I attended offered three morning worship services, 7 a.m., 9:00 a.m. and 11:00 a.m. No matter what time a day you attended there was a crowd of people waiting to get their praise on and Sunday sermon to get them through the week.

I was Security Director and as you can imagine, three services kept me and my team extremely busy. It was a delicate balance of protecting the House of God and its people without significantly interrupting or detracting from their worship experience. Even as my team and I worked, we could appreciate the Spirit filled atmosphere brought on by praise and worship, good singing and the day's sermon.

In the course of a day, the activities were almost non-stop. I knew that if things were going to run smoothly, it was critical to plan ahead and have the right people in place to get the job done. I am just a stickler for that sort of thing.

Romans 12:6-8 (NIV)

We have different gifts, according to the grace given to each of us. If your gift is prophesying, then prophesy in accordance with your[a] faith; if it is serving, then serve; if it is teaching, then teach; if it is to encourage, then give encouragement; if it is giving, then give generously; if it is to lead,[b] do it diligently; if it is to show mercy, do it cheerfully.

DON'T SKIP THE PROCESS

1 Peter 4:10-11 (NIV)

Each of you should use whatever gift you have received to serve others, as faithful stewards of God's grace in its various forms. If anyone speaks, they should do so as one who speaks the very words of God. If anyone serves, they should do so with the strength God provides, so that in all things God may be praised through Jesus Christ. To him be the glory and the power for ever and ever. Amen.

Even in the midst of preparing for details and services, God used me to reach people that I would come into contact with along the way. I remember how some parents would seek me out because they were having problems with their child at home or school. They expected me to talk with their child and issue a stern warning designed to get them back on track. I was always happy to help in this way because I viewed it as assignments from God. God's gifts to me had allowed me to encourage and speak to people of all ages in such a way that they were receptive to the messages received. No matter how busy I was, I always made time to serve God's purpose in this manner.

Whenever I spoke to young people I would *talk* to them, *not* at them. I also didn't sugarcoat the truth in discussing the conflict confronting them. I think young people appreciate straight talk just as much as adults when dealing with a situation.

My background as a police officer helped me to explain how a young person's choices in life determined what kind of future they could expect. Society judged them according to their behavior, and if they weren't careful it could have a long lasting negative effect which could follow them through adulthood. I encouraged children to listen to their parents because they wanted what was best for them. I'm sure that a lot of what I said to the children I counseled was nearly identical to what their parents had said. Sometimes a message gets lost because a person chooses to ignore the messenger, no matter how good the advice is.

I thank God that He used me in such a way that the message took root and made a positive difference in lives.

One Sunday morning, I was standing outside the church grounds just before the start of 11:00 a.m. service. I saw a young man *(late teens)* and a woman walking up the pathway to enter the church. As the two got closer to the church, the young man hesitated and then stopped. The woman sensing something was wrong, asked if he was coming in. "No," he said. "Why are you going in? I asked. I was curious as to why the young man would come this far just to turn around. His reply was that his mom was always trying to get him to believe in Jesus. Just as I had assumed, the woman he was with, was his mother. "Do you believe in Jesus?" I asked. He responded with a question of his own, "How can I believe in someone I never met?"

After hearing the direction our conversation was headed, his mother kept on walking and disappeared inside the church. I remained outside and questioned him further. I asked him again what his relationship was to the woman. With a smirk on his face, he said, "I already told you that she's my mom." Little did he know, that I had intentionally asked about their relationship for a reason.

Next, I asked him if he knew his mom's mother. With a sharp tongue he said, "Yeah, I know my grandmother."

DON'T SKIP THE PROCESS

I then asked him if he knew his mother's grandmother. Surprisingly, he stayed around long enough to continue the conversation. He said, "Yeah, I know about my mother's grandmother, but she's dead now."

I quickly asked if he had ever met her and he said, no because she died when he was a baby. I asked him if he knew a lot about his great grandmother. "Yeah," he replied. I said to him, so, you believe everything that was said about her? And you guessed it. Once again, his answer was, "Yeah." I then said to him, "You never actually met her, but you believe in her because of what your mother and grandmother told you, right?" In other words, you met her through the stories your mother and grandmother shared with you, and you believe their stories to be true, correct?" He stood there looking at me, trying to figure out where I was going with this.

It's the same with Jesus Christ," I told him. "You have never met Jesus in person, but through the reading of

DON'T SKIP THE PROCESS

His Word, the Bible...He stood there as I continued. "Your mom is the one who is the beginning of your future. She is leading you in the right direction because she believes in God's teachings and his love for us. In that manner, think about how she cares and provides for you." I continued speaking about the importance of getting to know Jesus, accepting and believing in Him. Before I could finish another sentence the young man walked away and towards the entrance of the church. As if I didn't know, I asked, "Where are you going?" He stopped and turned back my way. Without a word, he quickly turned back again and went inside the church. That was God's process at work. He used me to reach that young man. I am glad I didn't "skip that process."

Jesus taught us two of the greatest commandments. First, love the Lord your God with all your heart and with all your soul and with all your mind. And second, love your neighbor as yourself. *(Matthew 22:38 NIV)*

There are so many people walking around who are discouraged and lack a relationship with Jesus. Whatever gifts God has blessed you with should be used to assist others and draw them closer to our Lord and Savior Jesus Christ.

Opportunities arise on a daily basis to be a positive influence in the lives of others and help draw them to Christ. When you think no one is watching is exactly the time when you are being watched. Be a role model or example for how being a child of God positively impacts your life and the lives of others. How you interact with others and treat them will truly let them know if God is in you and the fruits of the spirit.

Are you using the gifts God has blessed you with so that you can truly be a blessing to others?

God's Process Being Used In
and Through Me

_____

_____

_____

_____

_____

_____

_____

_____

_____

_____

_____

_____

_____

God's Process Being Used In
and Through Me

_____

_____

_____

_____

_____

_____

_____

_____

_____

_____

_____

_____

_____

_____

THE YO-YO AFFECT

The yo-yo is one of the oldest toys in history. It has provided numerous generations of children and adults with hours of fun. Today you can still find yo-yos on store shelves. The simple design of this toy is a reel with a long string attached to the middle. Once you attach the string to your index finger, yu can roll the reel up and down by manipulating the string. If you are really good with the yo-yo you can make it do tricks, such as walking the dog or any number of more complex moves.

DON'T SKIP THE PROCESS

One day I decided to test a theory about how adults viewed operating a yo-yo. Mind you, it wasn't because I was obsessed with yo-yos. I was more interested in learning how a person's perspective on this might affect how they approach situations in life.

I approached several of my colleagues and asked each one what they considered to be the most important part of the yo-yo, the reel or the string. As you can imagine, I got all kinds of strange looks and questions before they decided to play along. Each person I spoke with replied, "the string." Each one considered the string important because it controlled the yo-yos movements. So, control was the most important factor they attributed to the string in operating a yo-yo. I can see why they would think this. Once you tie the string onto your finger and tighten it, it gives you the impression of control. By working your fingers you can move the yo-yo in any direction you choose.

DON'T SKIP THE PROCESS

While I could understand this view, I reminded them that sometimes the yo-yo doesn't return to you when you release it. Then you are forced to bend down and rewind it. At other times the yo-yo becomes detached from the string and rolls across the floor. What happened to the string's control in those instances? The yo-yo behaved in an unexpected way instead of following a pattern.

I think the yo-yo effect shows our natural tendency to want control over every aspect of our lives. We believe that if we take control of a situation or steps needed to complete a process that we can control the outcome. This isn't necessarily a bad thing, because setting goals and working to achieve them is a positive thing.

It becomes a problem when we mistakenly believe that having control will always bring us the desired results we want in life. As we all know, life doesn't operate that way. The unexpected can happen at any time and quickly leave us scrambling *(like the yo-yo rolling across the floor)* to try and fix things or make alternate plans. We may have little or no control over things like sickness, accidents, or the loss of a job, for example. We can only try to control our reaction to life's surprises and disruptions. When we fail to do this we are setting ourselves up for continued anxiety, stress and even chronic health problems. Learn to accept the fact that you will never be fully in control of everything that affects you. Only God, in His infinite wisdom and grace has that power. Trust that no matter what situation arises, you can get through it with God's help. Have faith that He can provide you with the strength and courage needed to weather any storm that passes your way. You will breathe a sigh of relief when you stop trying to do God's job and let Him have His way in your life.

THE LORD'S PRAYER

Psalm 23 (KJV)

The LORD is my shepherd; I shall not want.

He maketh me to lie down in green pastures: he leadeth me beside the still waters.

He restoreth my soul: he leadeth me in the paths of righteousness for his name's sake.

Yea, though I walk through the valley of the shadow of death, I will fear no evil: for thou art with me; thy rod and thy staff they comfort me.

Thou preparest a table before me in the presence of mine enemies: thou anointest my head with oil; my cup runneth over.

DON'T SKIP THE PROCESS

Surely goodness and mercy shall follow me all the days of my life: and I will dwell in the house of the LORD for ever.

The Yo-Yo Affect

_____

_____

_____

_____

_____

_____

_____

_____

_____

_____

_____

_____

_____

The Yo-Yo Affect

_____

_____

_____

_____

_____

_____

_____

_____

_____

_____

_____

_____

_____

_____

_____

_____

_____

KEEP YOUR EYES ON THE PRIZE

10

For those who love sports as I do, you enjoy watching the game, whether its baseball, football, basketball, soccer, golf, or some other game, there is usually a ball involved which is central to the sport. In order to win the game it is important to "keep your eye on the ball." Most games also require players to pay equal attention to the defense and offense. Know that as each player plays his role protecting his team's points or advancing them by scoring more, awareness of where the ball is at all times is critical. Regardless of which position you hold, the objective is to outsmart your opponent by blocking, checking, faking moves or actually tackling them down to gain the advantage. In baseball, the pitcher tries to "fake out" the batter by throwing different kinds of pitches that are unexpected. You have the curve ball that looks as if it's coming straight at you, but all of a sudden, it changes course and takes a quick curve in front of your very eyes.

Luke 18:1 (KJV)

And he spake a parable unto them to this end, that men ought always to pray, and not to faint;

THE CURVE BALL:

Watch the curve of life. Sometimes a bad situation looks as if it is coming right at you. During those times, but you call on the Lord with a powerful prayer on your lips. Before you know it, your problem can veer off into a different direction just like that curve ball did. You thought you were going to get hit by a storm, but it passed right on by you because of your faith in God's power.

THE FASTBALL:

You know it's coming so you dig your heels in and time your swing to "connect," but to no avail. You still missed it. That's because it came at you so fast, that you froze at the very moment that you should have been swinging. Scratching your head in disbelief, you wonder how you missed when you knew it was coming.

Life is like that sometimes. You may find yourself in situations where people and things come at you so fast that you feel unprepared to deal with it.

Even with the best of preparation, you may still feel overwhelmed or unsure of yourself. It is natural to worry about such things, but it's important not to let fear control you and prevent you from reaching your destiny.

If you're not prepared, hesitate in what you are seeking or are slow to move, you'll miss out on opportunities that were meant for you. There are too many times when a failure to act or make a decision results in a person missing out on a new job or promotion, gaining a spot on a new team, or even meeting the "right person" that you'd like to marry someday; whatever it is, there is a process to making it work for you.

Figure out what is important to you in life. Set goals for yourself. If you believe it, you can achieve it. Now actually start working to make your goals and dreams a reality. Believe it, then declare it by making positive statements and taking positive steps towards that goal. It is impossible to be successful if you have a self-defeated attitude. So, instead of saying why you can't achieve something, think of the ways you can make it happen and then diligently work towards it.

Job 22:28 (KJV)

Thou shalt also decree a thing, and it shall be established unto thee: and the light shall shine upon thy ways.

THE SLIDER BALL:

The slider is, and does just what it says; it slides right pass. It will throw you off your stride. Moving too quickly or too slowly to respond will cause you to miss the mark. How you react determines whether you will be successful or not.

Life an be that way was well. You meet people and become friends and expect the best of them and from them, but soon you begin to realize, that some were just a thorn in your side. They can always point out the negatives in your life and offer no real support. This constant emphasis on "what's wrong" instead of providing constructive feedback and assistance only devalues and hurts you. You become so discouraged that you give up on trying to improve yourself or your circumstances. When you realize this, it is best to cut ties and move on. You deserve better. Sometimes even the best of friendships may be affected by jealousy. Try to keep everything in perspective. True friends will remain loyal and stand by you even in bad times.

Your blessings can cause some people to become "haters." Instead of being happy for you, they may try to find your weaknesses and manipulate you for their own gain. They warn you to be wary of other people and not get too close, while at the same time they are plotting how to undermine you. Similar to the slider ball, this type of person slides right past your defenses by gaining your trust and then abusing it. Get in the habit of making good decisions and learn to trust your instincts. You will be surprised at the impact it has on your life.

Proverbs 3:5-6 (KJV)

Trust in the LORD with all thine heart; and lean not unto thine own understanding. In all thy ways acknowledge him, and he shall direct thy paths.

THE BASKETBALL:

The game is fun to play as well as to watch. Players dribble the basketball up and down the court trying to make a basket and score points. Your team also has to play defense to stop your opponent from scoring more points and winning the game. You have set plays designed for both offense and defense. The game is a process of set plays but we all know all too well, it doesn't always go as planned. Even the best players in the league expect to maintain control of the ball as they're dribbling it. These players must keep their eyes on the ball and prevent their opponents from stealing the ball.

Sometimes when a player dribbles the ball, it doesn't always come right back up as expected. It may hit someone else's foot and go in a different direction. The defender might swipe it away from them or they might hit a slippery spot and simply lose control of it. Even if the defensive player in front of you isn't watching the ball closely enough, you better believe one of the other teammates are.

What represents your basketball in life? How are you going down life's road trying to maintain control of what

DON'T SKIP THE PROCESS

God has entrusted in your hands? The devil is a liar and will put obstacles in your way to block your shots. We have to be very careful of whose team we're on. One thing you don't want is a ball hugger. You know the person in front of you wants the ball. You're focused on watching him because he plays a tight game. While you are watching him, he has the same intense focus on you. However, his goal is to keep you distracted *(by watching him),* while his team member sneaks up behind you, grabs the ball and passes it off to an open team member. That's game, and you just got played *(outsmarted).* Now you're the one chasing after him to get back what he's stolen from you. Sometimes life operates the same way. You have trained so hard and know your routes and plays, but if you skip the process at hand, it may land you in a place, where you are totally lost.

DON'T SKIP THE PROCESS

Now you find out that it's harder and harder to get ahead in the game, *(of life that is)*. You have to shoot your jump shot or make your layup by putting in your guards. It's the last two minutes of the game now. Now it's you who's watching the ball in your opponents hand. He's watching it, watching you and your teammates. He got game, again. There appears to be nothing stopping him, nothing in his way, but wait...he slips on that dime shaped spot of sweat on the floor. The ball bounces right into the palm of your hands. At the three point line, you get the ball off just before the buzzer. Your teammate gets the re-bound, passes it to you, you run up and slam dunk it into the basket for the winning points. WOW. And why you ask?

True, the game is a game, but for a professional player, it's his career, a part of his lively hood. His finances from the sport is what he lives off of to support himself and his family. You, on the other hand, play it just for the sport, but you love to win, just like in life. The game win is minimal in your case, but in the game of life, there is much more at stake. Your Christian walk in this life and how you treat others is important. You have to keep your eyes on the prize of Salvation.

If you want victory, you can't skip over praying and believing God will make a way out of no way. Believe that God is your ALL and ALL. Watch how your life turn around for the better once you start activating the power of prayer.

Let the devil know, that no matter how many balls may have slipped by you, that with God on your side you will never be benched.

Luke 21:36 (KJV)

Watch ye therefore, and pray always, that ye may be accounted worthy to escape all these things that shall come to pass, and to stand before the Son of man.

DON'T SKIP THE PROCESS

THE SOCCER BALL:

The soccer field is long and wide. The pace is always fast and even the best players get kicked and fall down. When players get injured, they still get up and continue to play unless the injury is too severe. When the injury is too great the player is carried off the field. Even when this happens the player's heart is still with the team and he or she inspires fellow teammates to play even harder, in homage to them.

One person stands at the goal and has to protect it. It really doesn't seem fair that one person has to protect such a wide distance and tall goal. You opponent's job is to kick the ball so quickly to his teammates you don't have time to catch up to it. Their teammate's intent is to stop it, control it and kick it even further away from you. No matter what moves they put on you, you have to steady your eyes on them, and not the ball when its in flight. If you don't it's going to sail past, right over your head. It always helps when you have reliable teammates.

Sometimes we find ourselves in positions where no matter how hard we work we continue to miss out or fall short of obtaining the goals we have set for ourselves. It seems especially unfair, when we see others who obtain their positions or gains without working hard or following the rules. When this happens, I believe God doesn't want us to get discouraged and give up. It may mean that there is something greater that He has in store for you. You would never change direction or course when needed, if everything came easily. Sometimes the very thing needed in our lives to improve it and push us to our greatest potential, is "change." The bottom line is that God wants us to keep on moving when things fail or don't turn out as we expected. Get the point? He doesn't want us to sit idly on the ground fixated on our problems. We also shouldn't begrudge others for their good fortune. God is able to do all things but fail and He ha more than an abundance of blessings for his children. For he wants us to faint not. Know that when we keep our eyes lifted towards heaven, we can reach our mark and make that goal. He said that it's okay for us to win the big prize, think big, pray big and receive big. You get the point?

Ephesians 3:20 (KJV)

Now unto him that is able to do exceeding abundantly above all that we ask or think, according to the power that worketh in us,

THE GOLF BALL:

The golf ball is small and plays many tricks. It can travel far and slice on you in a split second. Even though the

DON'T SKIP THE PROCESS

ball is small, when the swing and pressure is put behind it, the ball will travel high and far for a long distance. Amazing, isn't it how a tiny little golf ball can bring the winner such big financial gain. Many may not want to admit it, but it *is* a blessing for all professional ball players, to earn such phenomenal wages. If they invest and spend their money wisely; it continues to bless the players' families and communities, long after the players have passed and for many generations.

We know it doesn't always work out that way, and sometimes it is due to situations outside of the players' control. Some players are poor stewards of what God has blessed them with. They waste money and spend it unwisely. Such players spend money on everybody to impress people with their wealth or importance.

They set out purchasing houses, cars, private jets, boats and materialistic things instead of investing.

DON'T SKIP THE PROCESS

The main point I want to make in my goal ball comparison is this; it's amazing how you can do a whole lot with a little, especially when you are determined and remain focused on achieving your goals.

By now you're getting the point of why it is so critical that you learn to keep your eyes on the ball, right? Know this, it's up to you how you win the game. Whether you score the winning run, goal or touchdown will depend on your actions.

Don't be a spectator watching from the bench. You have to take some ownership over the decisions you make, and in determining how they will affect your own life.

1 Corinthians 15:58 (KJV)

Therefore, my beloved brethren, be ye stedfast, unmoveable, always abounding in the work of the

Lord, forasmuch as ye know that your labour is not in vain in the Lord.

Matthew 6:33 (KJV)

But seek ye first the kingdom of God, and his righteousness; and all these things shall be added unto you.

Proverbs 16:3 (KJV)

Commit thy works unto the LORD, and thy thoughts shall be established.

DON'T SKIP THE PROCESS

Keep Your Eyes on the Prize

_____

_____

_____

_____

_____

_____

_____

_____

_____

_____

_____

_____

_____

_____

_____

Keep Your Eyes on the Prize

_____

_____

_____

_____

_____

_____

_____

_____

_____

_____

_____

_____

_____

_____

WHEN YOU HEAR THAT SWEET, SWEET SOUND

11

I remember growing up in Detroit during the hot summer months. Sometimes it was simply too hot to play in the sun. On those days I opted to sit on the porch if there was a breeze. When that didn't work, I had to go inside to play or watch television. On of the most memorable sounds of my childhood was the music of an ice cream truck. It seemed like I had a tracking device because no matter how far it was in the distance, I immediately jumped up and paid attention. Oh yeah! The Mr. Frosty

DON'T SKIP THE PROCESS

Softee Ice Cream man was in the neighborhood. Well, the sound of music coming from the ice cream truck had the same effect on my brothers and sisters and every other neighborhood kid. No matter what we were doing, we immediately stopped and were drawn to the truck; visions of ice cream running through our heads.

Depending on where I was at the time, I would either jump off the front porch or rush through the front door, letting it slam loudly behind me. I would run to the sidewalk, watching and waiting for the ice cream truck to come into view. All I needed was just a glimpse of the truck; so I could time it. I knew just how much time was needed to run and ask momma for change and be back before the ice cream truck passed our house. The closer the ice cream man got the more excited everyone grew. You don't quite see the same fascination for ice cream that we had back then because ice cream trucks are rare nowadays.

DON'T SKIP THE PROCESS

It really is rare to see ice cream trucks in today's society. Most people purchase ice cream at the grocery store or visit a local ice cream parlor.

Another sound that caught our attention, was the loud sirens and fire engines. We lived near a fire station and could often hear the sirens as the firefighters made their runs. As young children, the idea that it meant danger for the person or persons involved was almost an afterthought. We were more fascinated by the excitement of it all; the flashing lights, stretchers, water hoses and ladders.

As an adult, the sirens that once fascinated me as a child now have a different meaning. I am more conscious of the danger present to first responders and the people they are assisting. My main concern now, is for a positive outcome. I am less concerned about the excitement of events taking place. This is a part of the process of growing up. You develop mentally and physically, and begin to look at things differently. Your whole perspective on life changes. Even your priorities change as you reach a different level of maturity.

What sticks out in my mind, is how much importance and attention we place on certain sounds that were familiar and special to us. We don't see the same type of fascination or attention being paid now because there are too many "distractions." People of all ages are busy doing too many things at once. Haven't you seen a person texting on the cell phone with the television on in the background while also listening to music on another device? You probably have a few examples yourself of how you have multi-tasked while working on several different assignments and devices. "What's wrong with that,?" you ask. Too many distractions can ovorwhclm the senses and lead you to falsely believe you're being productive. In reality, you're trying to do so much at once that something inevitable gets shortchanged by the lack of attention. When your mind is so preoccupied with the constant distractions of visual and audio eye candy available you begin to "tune out" everything else.

As a believer in Jesu Christ, I know that the Holy Spirit is God's presence in me, sent to comfort and protect me. There have been times I acted in a way that I hadn't planned and avoided danger *(unknown to me at the time)* in the process. Some people may call it instinct which causes them to react in a way they ordinarily wouldn't have and avoid trouble. I believe it is divine intervention which causes me to act in such a way.

DON'T SKIP THE PROCESS

Romans 8:28 (NIV)

And we know that in all things God works for the good of those who love him, who have been called according to his purpose.

Psalm 91:9-11 (NIV)

If you say, "The LORD is my refuge," and you make the Most High your dwelling, no harm will overtake you, no disaster will come near your tent. For he will command his angels concerning you to guard you in all your ways;

I have seen and experienced some things in my personal life that can only be explained as miracles. When God performs these miracles in our lives and the in our lives and in the lives of others we should never be ashamed to acknowledge His presence and give Him the glory.

I know today that the "sweet, sweet sound" we should all be listening for is God's voice and presence in our lives. He shouldn't have to compete with anything else to make us stop and pay attention. We strengthen our spiritual connection to God by reading and studying His Word revealed in the Bible. Building and strengthening your relationship with God is the best thing you can ever do. You will be surprised at how much easier it is to face whatever challenges life throws your way.

Imagine if we reacted to learning about the teachings of Jesus Christ, as children once did when hearing the sounds of the ice cream truck. We would run excitedly through the streets and neighborhoods telling everyone we ran into how wonder He is.

DON'T SKIP THE PROCESS

Don't be afraid to tell others your testimonies of just how good God has been to you. Sharing your testimonies of how God helped you overcome your trials reminds us all of God's grace, mercy and love for us all. Isn't it time to strengthen your relationship with God, so that you too wait with anticipation and excitement for the sweet, sweet sound of His voice speaking to you?

If you haven't already done so, NOW is the time to accept Jesus Christ as your Lord and Savior. The more you study the teachings of Jesus Christ, the closer you will grow towards Him and fulfilling your purpose in life.

DON'T SKIP THE PROCESS

Psalm 34:8 (KJV)

O taste and see that the LORD is good: blessed is the man that trusteth in him.

The best thing about the flavor of the Lord, is that it never goes stale, but lasts forever. Have you ever been to church or in the presence of someone who had a life-changing story to tell? I call these testimonies when the person is describing how God miraculously intervened on their behalf.

You can fell chills run through your body as they explained what could only be God's supernatural power in action. Chills begin to mix with tears of joy because it reminds you of how truly amazing God is. You're also reminded of the miracles He has performed in your own life. His Spirit spills all over you and fills you up with emotion. That's because God designed us to praise and worship Him. Sometimes, we get so caught up and full of ourselves that we try to take the credit for something that had absolutely nothing to do with us. You can't do that with miracles because by definition they are considered humanly impossible. I wouldn't even try to explain it with science. You just know it when you see it. The Holy Spirit in you rejoices when you realize that the young child who survived a plane crash that killed everyone else was impossible, but for God. Thoughts turn to your own near death experiences that many people in similar circumstances didn't survive. You *know* it was God covering you in the protection of His blood and surrounding you with angels to protect you. There is no shame in rejoicing in the awesome power and greatness of God.

I doubt if we'll ever have trucks wailing out the sweet name Jesus, in our life. That means it is up to each of us to be a witness for Christ. We don't need music blaring trucks or bullhorns to tell people about the goodness of God. Shout and praise the sweet name of Jesus to anyone who is willing to listen; and I mean "shout" figuratively.

You shouldn't be ashamed to speak openly about your belief in Jesus Christ. At the same time, you don't beat people over the head with your beliefs, hoping to wear them down to your point of view. Jesus, Himself never acted this way. He let His teachings and demeanor speak for Him. People willingly chose to learn more about His faith.

In the same way, it's up to us to be followers of Christ and lead by example. That is one of the best ways to introduce people to Christ. They see Him reflected in how you behave and treat others, it gains their attention and respect.

DON'T SKIP THE PROCESS

Matthew 5:16 (KJV)

Let your light so shine before men, that they may see your good works, and glorify your Father which is in heaven.

Philippians 2: 11 (KJV)

And that every tongue should confess that Jesus Christ is Lord, to the glory of God the Father.

Mark 16:15 (KJV)

And he said unto them, Go ye into all the world, and preach the gospel to every creature.

DON'T SKIP THE PROCESS

It is up to each of us to be an example for the teachings of Jesus Christ as shown in the Bible. There are so many ways to spread the gospel about Jesus Christ, especially with all of the new technology available today.

Please don't keep the goodness of Jesus Christ to yourself, or as a secret. So many people are needlessly struggling because they don't know Him. You have it within your power to introduce them to Jesus and Salvation.

When You Hear that Sweet, Sweet Sound

_____

_____

_____

_____

_____

_____

_____

_____

_____

_____

_____

_____

_____

_____

_____

_____

_____

When You Hear that Sweet, Sweet Sound

_____

_____

_____

_____

_____

_____

_____

_____

_____

_____

_____

_____

_____

_____

THE SIGNAL OF A WHISPER

12

Outside of our daily prayers, there are times when a special needs prayer is needed. We get down on our knees and pray that God will answer our prayers in deliverance from whatever is troubling us. When we get up, we feel good about His hearing our plea, but we may not see the immediate results we were expecting. We continue praying over and over. As days and nights go by we may still not see the results we were expecting, and we get discouraged. There are times in life when no amount of fasting or prayer will get you the thing you requested. Think about it; was it a selfless prayer or a selfish one? Perhaps your prayer *(while well-meaning)* for God to extend someone's life is prolonging their agony. There are times when we ask God for things that are outside of His will. When that happens, we have to trust that in His infinite wisdom He knows what is best for us and the situation we are facing. God's knowledge and way of thinking is on a level which is incomprehensible to us.

1 Corinthians 10:13 (KJV)

No temptation has overtaken you except what is common to mankind. And God is faithful; he will not let you be tempted[b] beyond what you can bear. But when you are tempted, he will also provide a way out so that you can endure it

DON'T SKIP THE PROCESS

Sometimes it is difficult for us to accept that God knows what's best for us. In our grief or disappointment, we may turn away from God. We may start to have doubts about him and begin to complain or even falter in our faith. This is how the devil operates, sowing seeds of distrust and trying to lead us away from God.

Holding on to old wounds, hate, resentment or grudges feeds into the devil's plan to destroy you and your relationship with God. Don't be deceived by this trick. Try to remain unwavering in your faith like Job did when faced with incredible odds and trials. Job knew that no matter how difficult things had become in his life, that God wouldn't abandon him if he remained faithful. He was right. Continue praying and studying the Bible. Surround yourself with people who help strengthen your faith in God, not destroy it.

DON'T SKIP THE PROCESS

The Bible tells us to be slow to speak but quick to listen. If you have never heard the whisper of God, then it's time to get into a great Bible based church where you're taught to read, study and apply the Word of God to your life. Maybe you're the one who isn't listening because you haven't prepared yourself to actually hear what God is telling you and placing on your heart. You should learn to be a doer *(practice it)* as well as hearer of His Word. People should be able to look at how you act and treat others, for sure, to know that you're a child of God and a believer in His Word.

Parents expect their children to learn the basic academics of school such as English, math and science. They also expect their children to learn life skills that will help them to develop and serve them well throughout lives. A well-rounded education is considered one of the best tools to helping our children become successful in life and society. When children do well in life, it makes things a lot easier on us as their parents, knowing that we did something right.

God also want His children to do well. He has provided His Word (the Bible) to guide us, and give us the ultimate sacrifice of His son's blood so that we could be saved from our sins. God expects His children to also grow and develop in their faith.

We have a duty to teach others about the goodness of Christ and how to obtain salvation. You can help build the Kingdom of God by sharing the Word of God with those who are lost and in need of His presence in their lives. None of us are perfect, but God still loves us and wants what's best for His children. God, who is perfect in every way, knows that his children are less than perfect. For all have sinned and fallen short.

Despite this, God created a way to rescue us from our sins. He made the ultimate sacrifice of His son Jesus Christ's life so that we could have salvation. This is unconditional love which shows the awesome magnitude of God's grace and mercy towards His children. Have you ever been so busy playing outside that you didn't hear your mom when she called you from the porch? When you didn't respond she would raise her voice to make sure you weren't ignoring her. You didn't have to be a genius to know that if her tone of voice continued on this path that you would be in serious trouble. So you would immediately rush over to what your mom wanted.

Sometimes God also has to raise His voice or do something that will gain your attention and get you back on track. Whether God chooses to speak to you loudly or in the form of a whisper, He knows the best way to reach you so that you will be receptive. Are you ready to listen?

God blesses us by putting people in our path who can help us. He uniquely positions His children in such a way that no matter the circumstances they are assured victory if they remain faithful. God's favor upon your life opens doors that you thought were closed.

Remember the time that your friend came over, and in conversation, she tells you that her job is looking to hire someone with your worked skills. The two of you talk some more an she leaves. Later that evening she posts the job on Facebook, tagging you in it. You're so busy doing other things at the time that you forget to read the post. In the middle of the night, you become restless and can't sleep. You keep hearing the low beeping hum of your computer. You were sure you had turned it off. You get up to do that and see your friends posting from earlier in the day. You stare at it for a while and think, I really should apply for this job, but I'm too sleepy. You reach to turn off the computer and it beeps even lower this time; the battery life is low because the plug has fallen out. You plug up the computer and it lights up the whole room with the posting included. You're so sleepy, but you need this job. So you sit down at the computer and complete the on-line job application before shutting down the computer and returning to bed. Two days later, you get a phone call about the job and are asked to come in for an interview. The interview goes so well that you are offered the position with benefits and a good starting salary. "WOW, NOBODY BUT GOD," you tell yourself because you recognize God's favor when you see it.

Everything worked together to put you in position to receive God's blessing. God sent you a messenger to tell you about the job opportunity. When you neglected to follow up right away, you felt an uneasy restlessness in your spirit. Despite your tiredness you couldn't go back to sleep until you had finished what God placed in your heart to do. He knew that you needed that job.

Now this was a hypothetical situation you just read, but think about the times in your own life that God showed up when you needed Him; those times that he opened up doors that were closed. I am talking about those times when God showed you favor like never before. Always remember to praise and thank God for the many blessings He has provided.

Romans 8:26-27 (NIV)

In the same way, the Spirit helps us in our weakness. We do not know what we ought to pray for, but the Spirit himself intercedes for us through wordless groans. And he who searches our hearts knows the mind of the Spirit, because the Spirit intercedes for God's people in accordance with the will of God.

Help people when you can and encourage them. You have a great responsibility to be a good steward with what God has blessed you with. When you do that, you multiply the blessing in such a way that God's power and goodness can be seen and felt by many.

Remember the two fish and five loaves of bread that Jesus received to feed a hungry crowd? He didn't grumble or complain that it wasn't enough. The Bible says He looked towards Heaven and gave thanks to His Father before breaking the bread. God's blessing multiplied 2 fish and 5 loaves into a meal that was able to feed a multitude of people. (*Luke 9:16 KJV*)

You have a duty to spread the news of how good God is, so that others can seek Him and develop their own relationship with Him. Let your light so shine, so that others can see the goodness of God in you. This is

DON'T SKIP THE PROCESS

something you need to grasp with everything that is in

you. You MUST be the example people need to see.

It is our job to tell the world about God. Be the beacon

of light set on a hill that cannot be hid. Pay attention to

what God is trying to say to tell you and to the direction

He is pulling you towards. Whether He reaches you by

a soft whisper or a booming noise, only He knows the

best way to talk to His child. We can avoid so much

trouble if we'd only take the time to listen to God and

wait on Him instead of trying to solve problems

ourselves.

Sometimes that signal or message from God will come

in a still whisper to you, meant for your ears only.

Study the Word of God. Daily. When you know the

Word of God for yourself, you will not be deceived by

the enemy. Just remember that God is not the author

of confusion. Believing in Him and listening to Him will

never result in your mind being clouded or disoriented because He is a God or order.

Acts 17:11 (KJV)

These were more noble than those in Thessalonica, in that they received the word with all readiness of mind, and searched the scriptures daily, whether those things were so.

Know that obeying the whisper of God will keep you cover by the blood and not cover in blood, you own.

DON'T SKIP THE PROCESS

The Signal of a Whisper

_____

_____

_____

_____

_____

_____

_____

_____

_____

_____

_____

_____

_____

_____

_____

_____

DON'T SKIP THE PROCESS

The Signal of a Whisper

YOUR CHANCE TO LEAVE A MESSAGE

13

Have you ever heard your phone ring and wonder

who's calling? You take a peek at the phone but don't

recognize the number. What if it's another one of those

unsolicited telemarketing calls that no one likes? You

make a split second decision not to answer it and not

let the call go to voicemail. For anyone who has been

in this situation, you sometimes find that the caller fails

to leave a voicemail message at all. So, the caller still

remains a mystery.

DON'T SKIP THE PROCESS

Sometimes when you are calling on the name of Jesus you may feel like you're not getting an answer. Maybe it's because He's waiting on you to leave a message since He hasn't heard your voice in a while.

God has been trying to reach you, but you fail to pick up and you ignore His calls. Maybe it was an unexpected sign on a billboard that caught your attention, or perhaps a dream that sticks with you.

The point is that God sends messages in many ways. If you're not open and receptive you can miss the message that He has especially for you.

Romans 10:17 (KJV)

So then faith cometh by hearing, and hearing by the word of God.

DON'T SKIP THE PROCESS

Many of us wait until something tragic happens before we call on God. We should pray continually despite the circumstances. He is deserving of praise and worship for so many good things that have happened in our lives. I believe that God doesn't want a part-time relationship with us. He wants us to communicate with him during the good times and the bad times.

If you doubt the importance of prayer or the power of prayer then you weren't paying close attention to the example Jesus set for us. Jesus always reserved time to spend with His Father in prayer. He would find a quiet place where He could communicate in peace and He strengthened his prayer experience by fasting.

Jesus told us that faith the size of a mustard see could move mountains. *(Matthew 18:20 KJV).* Can you imagine a mustard seed which is smaller than a pencil eraser moving something as large as a mountain? (a situation so huge and overwhelming.) faith activates prayer and turns the impossible into the possible.

Let Jesus know you Love him, need him, adore him, will serve him, the Most High God. Accept him as your Lord and Savior Jesus Christ on a FULL-TIME basis, not just when the storms of life arise. Oftentimes, when we do call on God, we expect an answer right away. When we don't get it, we wonder if He even heard our prayer. Well, he does. We are a "want it right now" type of people, having no time to study to show ourselves approved; even worthy of a return. It is important to find time to study His Word. After all, the Bible is life's instruction manual. It has all the answers.

Want a return call? Leave a message especially if it has been a long time. Identify yourself. Make sure He knows that it's you that's calling. Jesus will return your message, but in his timing, which is ALWAYS on time.

DON'T SKIP THE PROCESS

It's nice to show a person how much you love him or her by your actions. You can do everything under the sun that shows you care, but every now and then, they still want to hear you say the words. God knows your heart, but He still wants to see your love for Him represented in your actions as well as your words.

Hebrews 11:1 (KJV)

Now faith is the substance of things hoped for, the evidence of things not seen.

So don't dial God up and get angry just because He doesn't answer when *you* expected it. He's been waiting for so long to hear from you, so when you do call on Him, leave him a straight forward message.

Believe me when I say, God *will* return your call. Just you be ready to answer.

DON'T SKIP THE PROCESS

Your Chance to Leave a Message

_____

_____

_____

_____

_____

_____

_____

_____

_____

_____

_____

_____

_____

_____

_____

DON'T SKIP THE PROCESS

Your Chance to Leave a Message

_____

_____

_____

_____

_____

_____

_____

_____

_____

_____

_____

_____

_____

_____

_____

_____

IT'S NOT WHAT'S ON YOU BUT WHAT'S IN YOU

14

Uniforms can tell us a lot about a person. Right away we know what type of job a person has and what skills are needed to do that job. Just a quick glance at the person's uniform or outward appearance tells us a lot about the person without having to have a conversation.

Even when people don't wear uniforms, we quickly form opinions about them based on what they are wearing. So there is a lot of emphasis and attention placed on outward appearance. It can help determine whether or not you get hired with a company. Outward appearance also tells people about your likes or dislikes because fashion can be an indicator of a person's personality.

It is important to dress for success when you are applying for school or a job, or anything else that you consider important. Your outward appearance should express confidence. Whether you like it or not, people will make assumptions about you based on what you wear. It is human nature. Sometimes these assumptions are accurate and sometimes they are completely off base. You should always dress to impress for the things that you consider important. What is equally important, *(if not more so)* is what's inside you. What is your attitude and behavior towards others like? If you are a person who only feels good when you belittle others and make them feel stupid, then you are likely to be lonely at some point.

DON'T SKIP THE PROCESS

People can't see your character and integrity by what you wear. We expect our soldiers, police officers, fire fighters and preachers to uphold those values because those traits are associated with the uniforms they wear. As anyone knows though, uniforms don't make a person good. The men and women who wear uniforms have to possess these qualities for you to see them action.

We should never overestimate the importance of outward appearance. Nor should we underestimate the importance of *(having and teaching)* character, integrity, dependability, compassion, and respect.

Jesus taught us that everyone is equal regardless of what position in life they hold. Everyone is deserving of respect and fair treatment even when they fail to pass our tests for outward appearance.

First impressions are what others see when they look at you. Unless they take the time to learn more about you

DON'T SKIP THE PROCESS

they may never know how nice or honest you are.

When you put on a uniform your conduct should speak for you because of who you are, not because of what you are wearing. Let your actions speak for you in everything you do, and learn not to judge people for superficial reasons. Remain proud and true to yourself no matter what profession you hold.

DON'T SKIP THE PROCESS

It's Not What's On You But What's In You

_____

_____

_____

_____

_____

_____

_____

_____

_____

_____

_____

_____

_____

_____

DON'T SKIP THE PROCESS

It's Not What's On You But What's In You

_____

_____

_____

_____

_____

_____

_____

_____

_____

_____

_____

_____

_____

_____

_____

_____

Conclusion

It has been said that it is not how you start but how you finish; however, you can't finish something if you haven't started. Don't let fear, anxiety, worry or doubts prevent you from achieving your dreams. When you have confidence in yourself you are capable of great things, especially when you follow the path God has set you on and continually seek His guidance.

Now go out there and **SOAR** as high as you can by being a bright and positive influence in your homes, churches, workplace and communities.

Be blessed and stay focused!

ADDITIONAL NOTES

ADDITIONAL NOTES

_____

_____

_____

_____

_____

_____

_____

_____

_____

_____

_____

_____

_____

_____

_____

DON'T SKIP THE PROCESS

Herbert Brown's Biography

Herbert Brown is the youngest of 9 children born to parents James F. Brown, Sr. and Patricia Ann King-Brown. He has been married for 25 years and has two daughters.

Herbert became a Professional Security Consultant after retiring from the Detroit Police Department. His expertise in providing risk assessment and loss prevention services has helped businesses to thrive by minimizing losses to profitability and ensuring the safety of personnel and members of the community. He enjoys motivational speaking and encouraging others to live life to their fullest potential.

DON'T SKIP THE PROCESS

The dynamic leader has worked with numerous celebrities, community leaders and politicians.

Highlights of his career include providing executive protection security for President Obama while he was still a Senator and guest speaker at the Detroit NAACP Freedom Fund Dinner in 2005.

Don't Skip the Process is Herbert's first book. It is a motivational self-help book which shares his own challenges and how he overcame them to be successful. Herb draws upon his own personal and professional experience and how he has inspired others to overcome challenges and achieve their dreams.

DON'T SKIP THE PROCESS

Made in the USA
Monee, IL
14 June 2021